Usborne Facts of Life
Growing up

Susan Meredith

Designed by Nancy Leschnikoff and Roger Priddy

Illustrated by Sue Stitt, Kuo Kang Chen, Verinder Bhachu, Emma Julings, Stephen Moncrieff, Nancy Leschnikoff, and Rob McCaig

Consultants: Judy Cunnington (Relate), Dr Fran Reader and Revd Professor Michael J. Reiss

Contents

About this book

You have been growing up since the day you were born. Just as a baby grows and changes as it becomes a child, so there is another, equally important, period of growth as you stop being a child and become an adult. This period is called adolescence.

Adolescence

Adolescence lasts for several years, from around age 11 or younger up to around 18 or older. It involves all kinds of changes, both to your mind and emotions (psychological changes) and to your body (physical changes). This book concentrates mainly on explaining the physical changes.

Growing

On the first few pages you will find out about growth and what changes you can expect in your body shape.

Puberty

The physical changes of adolescence are called puberty. Most of them take place in the early years of adolescence.

Pages 8-9 will give you a general idea of the changes of puberty, how they happen and when. Then, on the following pages, they are all explained in more detail.

Sex and babies

The most important change of all is that you start being able to produce children; so, on pages 17-37, there are sections on reproduction, sex, how contraception is used to prevent unwanted pregnancies, and on sexually transmitted infections.

Your emotions

Although this book deals mainly with the physical changes of adolescence, your emotions are very important too. Some of the confusing feelings you may experience are mentioned on page 51.

Finding out more

You will find further information about things that affect your body, such as food and drugs, on pages 38-50. At the end of the book there is a glossary and some telephone numbers which may be helpful.

The colours inside you

The illustrations in this book, including the photographs, show the insides of your body in different colours so you can see all the parts clearly. In reality, most of your insides are a brownish-red.

Growing

One of the first changes of puberty is that you suddenly grow taller very fast. This "growth spurt" is triggered by substances called hormones, which are made by glands in your body. You will find out more about them later.

During your growth spurt, you grow as fast as you did when you were two years old. When a boy is growing at his fastest, he usually adds 7-12cm (2¾-4¾in) to his height in a single year. Girls add 6-11cm (2¼-4¼in).

Height

At age 10...		At age 12...		At age 18...	
138cm (4ft 6in) 78%	138cm (4ft 6in) 84%	148cm (4ft 10in) 84%	150cm (4ft 10½in) 91%	177cm (5ft 9in) 100%	164cm (5ft 4in) 100%

These pictures show the average height of males and females at different ages and the percentage of their adult height that they have reached.

Girls start their growth spurt at about 10½ and boys at about 12½ so, for a while, girls tend to be taller than boys. Boys catch up by the time they are 13, though, and they still have some growing to do while girls have almost finished.

All the ages and figures given in this book are averages only. Growth in height, like every other change of puberty, varies from person to person. Your final height has nothing to do with when you start your growth spurt. It depends mainly on what you have inherited from your parents.

A few people don't go through a real growth spurt at all but just keep on getting taller very gradually instead.

How tall will you be?

You can use the information in the chart below to estimate how tall you will be once you have finally finished growing.

It tells you what percentage of your final height you are likely to have reached at any age during puberty.

Here is the calculation you need to do:

$$\frac{\text{Present height (cm or in)}}{\text{\% of full height (see chart)}} \times \frac{100}{1}$$

Here is an example for a boy, aged nine, who is 130cm tall:

$$\frac{130}{75} \times \frac{100}{1} = 173$$

This boy is likely to be about 173cm tall when he has finished growing.

Age	%	
	Boys	Girls
8	72%	77%
9	75%	81%
10	78%	84%
11	81%	88%
12	84%	91%
13	88%	95%
14	92%	98%
15	95%	99%
16	98%	99.5%
17	99%	100%
18	100%	100%

How bones grow

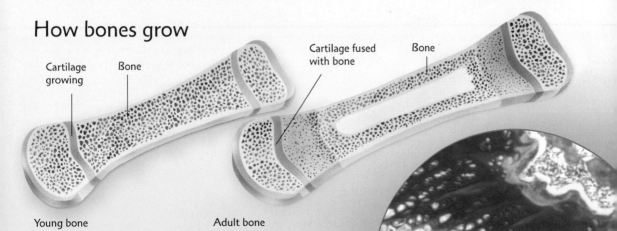

Cartilage growing

Bone

Cartilage fused with bone

Bone

Young bone

Adult bone

Long bones, like those in your arms and legs, contain a rubbery substance called cartilage near the ends. The bones grow longer as the cartilage grows. Eventually, under the influence of sex hormones, the cartilage fuses with the bone and you stop growing.

One of the reasons women are generally smaller than men is that they become sexually mature earlier and so have less time to continue growing.

This is a photograph of part of a long bone injected with dye. The dark blue diagonal band is growing cartilage.

Body shapes

As you grow taller, your body shape changes too. Females' hips get broader as their pelvic bones widen. This gives more room for a baby to grow and be born. Males usually develop broader shoulders, which gives them added strength.

Female pelvis

Male pelvis

Hips

Spine

Pelvic bone

Voice changes

As the rest of your body grows, your voice box (larynx) also gets bigger and this makes your voice deeper. Most people's voices change very gradually, but a few alter all at once. Males' voices go deeper than females' because males develop larger voice boxes. You can see this from the way their Adam's apple sticks out.

Boys are sometimes embarrassed during puberty by their voices suddenly breaking into a squeak. This happens when the muscles of their larynx get out of control just for a moment.

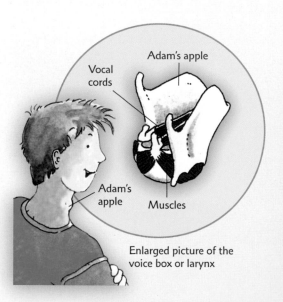

Vocal cords

Adam's apple

Adam's apple

Muscles

Enlarged picture of the voice box or larynx

Face changes

You will notice that your face alters quite a lot at puberty. Some people say it looks as though it is coming down from under the skull. Your nose and jaw both become more prominent and your hairline recedes. Boys' faces alter more than girls' do.

Child's skull

Adult's skull

Muscles

As you grow up, your muscles get bigger and you get stronger. At birth, around 20% of your body is muscle. This increases to around 25% in early puberty and around 40% when you are adult. Men tend to have more muscle than women relative to their size. It isn't true that you can "outgrow your strength" and so become weak and exhausted. Strength does lag behind size though, so you may look stronger than you really are for a while.

Why are men stronger than women?

Sometimes, men are stronger and have more stamina than women. This is not only because of their size, shape and muscles, but also because they develop larger hearts and lungs than women, relative to their size. The differences are often exaggerated by upbringing, if boys are encouraged to do more sports, for example, than girls. Being stronger doesn't make men healthier than women and, in fact, women usually live longer.

The "ideal" figure

Some people worry that they are not a certain shape or size. This is partly due to the "ideal" figures, especially of women, shown in the media. In reality, different people find different body types attractive and, provided you are not very over or under weight, you don't need to worry.

Feeling gangly

When you are going through your growth spurt, you don't grow at the same rate all over. First, your feet and hands get bigger, then your arms and legs lengthen and, about a year later, the rest of your body grows. This may not be noticeable but some people are conscious of having oversized hands and feet for a while.

What happens at puberty?

When you reach puberty, all sorts of changes start happening in your body. The main reason for them all is so that you are able to start having children, when you are older.

Important changes happen to your sex organs. These grow and develop, and start producing the special sex cells from which babies can be made.

(An organ is any part of your body with a particular job to do and a cell is the smallest individual living unit in your body.)

You aren't aware of some of the changes going on, because they take place right inside your body. Others are more obvious. The pictures below show the main changes of puberty.

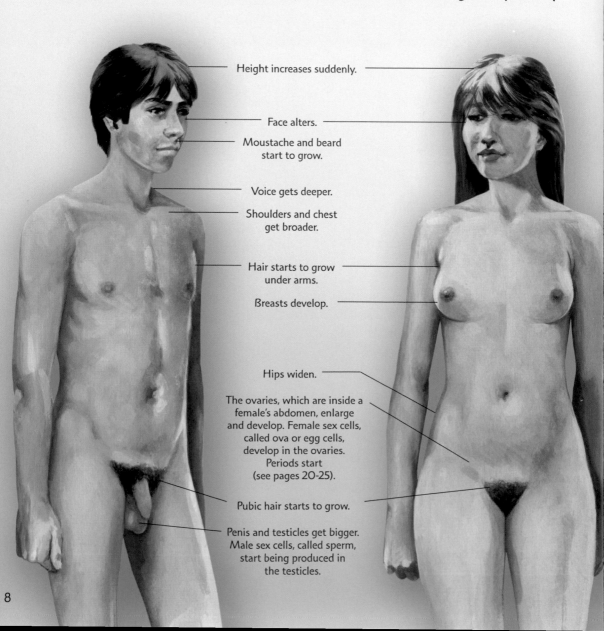

Height increases suddenly.

Face alters.

Moustache and beard start to grow.

Voice gets deeper.

Shoulders and chest get broader.

Hair starts to grow under arms.

Breasts develop.

Hips widen.

The ovaries, which are inside a female's abdomen, enlarge and develop. Female sex cells, called ova or egg cells, develop in the ovaries. Periods start (see pages 20-25).

Pubic hair starts to grow.

Penis and testicles get bigger. Male sex cells, called sperm, start being produced in the testicles.

When does puberty start?

The age when people reach puberty varies between the sexes and also between individuals. The average age is usually said to be 11 for girls and 13 for boys. This is misleading, though, because girls can reach puberty any time between 8 and 14, and boys any time between 10 and 16.

This large timespan means that two people of the same age can be very different. One of them may have finished developing physically before the other one has even started.

This sometimes causes embarrassment. It may help to know that neither "early" nor "late" development is in any way abnormal. Nor is one "better" than the other.

The age when you reach puberty doesn't affect what you will be like as an adult. Whether your body matures slowly or quickly, it will continue the process until you are fully developed.

What determines the age you reach puberty is partly the characteristics you've inherited from your parents. Your build may play a part too. People who are short and stocky tend to reach puberty earlier than tall, thin people.

Attraction

Some of the changes that happen at puberty, such as beard growth and breast development, are not essential for producing children.

Unlike the sex organs, which are primary sexual features, these are known as secondary sexual features. They are often attractive to the opposite sex, acting as a signal that you are different from them.

Changing times

Nowadays, people reach puberty younger than they used to. This is probably for a combination of reasons: children eat more than they used to, they eat different kinds of food, they have more body fat and get less exercise, and they have fewer diseases of the type which delay the start of puberty.

How puberty starts

The changes in your body during puberty all start in your brain and are caused by chemical substances called hormones. When you are a child, you have only low levels of certain hormones in your body and no one knows quite what they do.

At puberty, your brain increases the levels of these hormones and this makes your body start producing the sex cells: ova or sperm. The levels of other hormones, known as the sex hormones, also increase to bring about the rest of the changes of puberty.

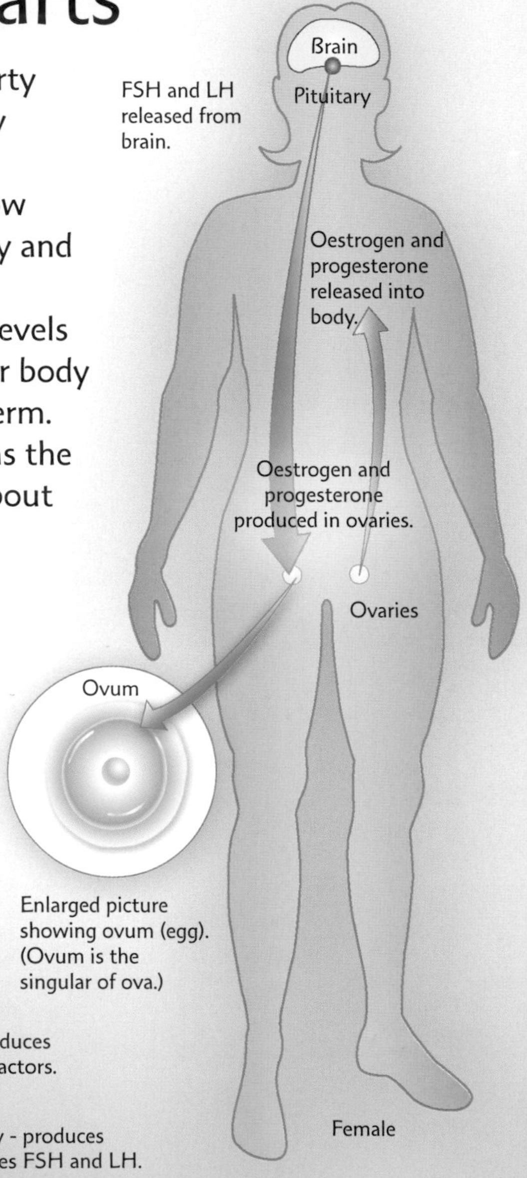

Your brain and puberty

Puberty starts in a tiny part of your brain called the hypothalamus. When this is developed enough, it starts sending high levels of hormones to another part of your brain, called the pituitary gland.

The hormones from the hypothalamus are known as "releasing factors" because they trigger the pituitary gland to start releasing higher levels of two other hormones, called FSH and LH.

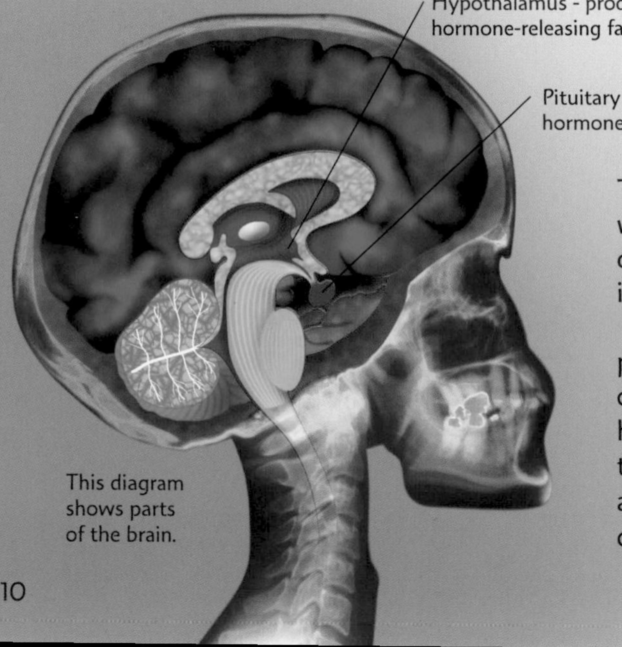

FSH and LH released from brain.

Brain

Pituitary

Oestrogen and progesterone released into body.

Oestrogen and progesterone produced in ovaries.

Ovaries

Ovum

Enlarged picture showing ovum (egg). (Ovum is the singular of ova.)

Female

Hypothalamus - produces hormone-releasing factors.

Pituitary - produces hormones FSH and LH.

This diagram shows parts of the brain.

The hormones FSH and LH make the ova which are in girls' ovaries begin to develop, and they start sperm production in boys' testicles.

The ovaries and testicles now start producing high levels of hormones of their own. These are the sex hormones. The sex hormones help the ovaries and testicles themselves to continue maturing and they also bring about the other, more obvious changes that happen to people at puberty.

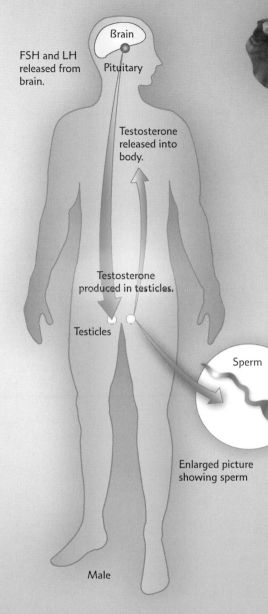

FSH and LH released from brain.

Brain

Pituitary

Testosterone released into body.

Testosterone produced in testicles.

Testicles

Sperm

Enlarged picture showing sperm

Male

Crystals of the male sex hormone, testosterone, magnified thousands of times and dyed. (In your body, hormones are greyish.)

What are hormones?

You have many other types of hormones in your body besides the ones to do with reproduction. Adrenalin, for example, is a hormone which prepares your body to take emergency action when you are feeling afraid or angry.

Hormones are produced in groups of cells called endocrine glands. The pituitary, for example, is an endocrine gland. The glands are attached to blood vessels which have thin walls. The hormones pass from the glands through the walls and into your blood. Your blood then carries them all around your body. Different hormones act on different parts of your body.

For example, they bring about the development of breasts in girls and the growth of beards in boys. The main female sex hormones are oestrogen and progesterone. The most important male sex hormone is testosterone.

The ovaries do not produce only female sex hormones but a low level of male ones as well. In the same way, the testicles produce low levels of female sex hormones as well as male ones.

This is a photograph of part of the endocrine gland called the thyroid, which is in your neck.

Blood vessel

Cells of thyroid gland

Hair

You grow hair on various parts of your body when you reach puberty. The hair growth is triggered by the sex hormones. Human beings are related to apes and the hair dates from a time when people were covered all over with fairly thick hair.

Pubic hair

This is hair which grows in the area of your external sex organs, or "genitals". The hair is a secondary sexual feature: although it isn't essential for reproduction, it draws attention to the genitals and is generally attractive to the opposite sex.

At first, pubic hair is fairly soft, but it eventually becomes coarser than the hair on your head, and curly. It is not unusual for pubic hair to be a completely different shade from the hair on your head.

Female pubic hair   Male pubic hair

Underarm hair

You usually start to get hair under your arms a year or two after your pubic hair begins to grow. No one really knows what purpose this hair has.

Some women remove the hair, using a razor or hair-removing cream, but there is no medical reason for doing this. You will not sweat any less and the hair soon grows back and has to be removed again.

If ever you use hair-removing cream, always follow the instructions that come with it very carefully, as the skin under your arms is very sensitive.

Hair on your body

Both males and females get longer hair on their arms and legs at puberty. Males in particular often get hair on their chests too and sometimes on their abdomen, shoulders, back, hands and feet.

Body hair shows up more on men than it does on women because it is thicker. If your hair is dark, it will show up more than if it is fair.

The amount of hair you get depends on what you have inherited from your parents. Having a lot of hair does not make a man more "manly" or a woman in any way "unwomanly" and it has nothing to do with sexual ability.

Although body hair is natural and normal, some people like to shave or use cream to remove it, especially from their legs. It is worth bearing in mind that the hair will grow back again, probably thicker than it was before.

Never try to dry-shave body hair. Razors need to be used with warm water and shaving foam or gel. Always follow the instructions with any hair-removing cream very carefully.

Comb

Beards

The growth of a beard and moustache is usually one of the last changes to happen to boys at puberty. First, hair grows on your upper lip, then on your cheeks and lastly on your chin. A lot of men have small hairless patches at the sides of their chin.

At first, the hair is soft but it gradually gets coarser. It is not necessarily the same shade as the hair on your head.

Some experts think men's beards are the equivalent of roosters' combs and that they are an important secondary sexual feature.

Shaving

Some boys feel slightly embarrassed when their beard begins to grow but you don't have to wait for a thick growth before you start shaving. On the other hand, you don't have to shave. If you decide to let your beard grow, make sure you keep it clean.

The quickest, most convenient way to shave is with an electric razor but many men find they get a closer, cleaner shave with foam or gel and warm water and a non-electric razor.

Start at one ear and work around to chin. Shave downwards in the direction of hairs or it may hurt.

Do other side of face, top lip, then under chin. For a closer shave, then try shaving upwards.

It is easier to cut yourself when you use a non-electric razor, though. Most men tend to shave in the way shown on the left.

Shaving in warm water opens up the pores of your skin. Splashing on cold water when you have finished helps to close them up again. Aftershave lotion contains astringents, which do the same thing, but they sting when you first put the lotion on. Too much aftershave can make your skin dry and flaky.

Girls and facial hair

Many girls get a fine covering of hair on their faces. It is not usually noticeable. If the hair is very dark and you are really unhappy about it, you can use cream to remove it or ask a beauty therapist about bleaching it. Don't try to shave, as the skin is more sensitive than boys' skin.

Stray hairs

You can find stray hairs growing anywhere on your body. Some people like to pluck them out or cut them off, especially if they are on their face.

It is better not to pluck a hair which is growing out of a mole in case it damages the mole; just cut the hair off instead.

Breasts

Developing breasts is one of the main changes of puberty for girls. The hormone oestrogen, produced by the ovaries, makes the breasts develop, starting usually around age 11 and continuing until full size is reached around age 17. Your nipples are the first things to grow.

As your breasts develop and enlarge, they may feel uncomfortable at times. Also, one breast may develop faster than the other. They will even out later, though no one's breasts match exactly. The age your breasts start developing has no bearing on their eventual size.

What are breasts for?

The main purpose of breasts is to produce milk for feeding any babies a woman might have. Breast milk is a baby's ideal first food.

Breasts are also an important secondary sexual feature. They are attractive to men and are sensitive to touch, which increases the woman's sexual pleasure.

Breast size

A lot of women worry that their breasts are either too big or too small. Like worries about general body shape, this may be due to images of "ideal" women shown in the media. In reality, all sizes of breasts are equally able to feed babies, as the size is determined by fat, not by the milk-producing or storing areas. Breasts are also equally sensitive, whatever their size, and men differ as to the size and shape they find most attractive.

Do exercises work?

No amount of exercising can increase your breast size, because exercise works by building up muscle and there are no muscles in breasts.

Exercise involving the chest muscles, such as swimming, will strengthen these muscles and may help them to support your breasts more easily.

Boys and breasts

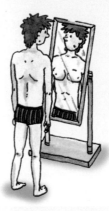

Some boys find that their breasts become tender or swell slightly at puberty. This is nothing to worry about. You are not changing sex and the "breasts" will disappear within about 18 months, as hormone production settles down.

What are breasts made of?

When a woman has a baby, a hormone from her pituitary gland triggers milk production in these parts of her breasts. The milk is made from substances which pass out of the woman's blood as it travels through the breasts.

Each breast contains 15 to 20 of these tubes or "ducts". In childhood, the ducts are very small but at puberty they enlarge and branch out. When milk is produced in the breasts after a woman has had a baby, it drains into the ducts and is stored there until the baby needs it.

The nipple is the most sensitive part of the breast. When it is stimulated by sensations such as touch or cold, tiny muscles around its base make it erect.

The shape of nipples varies, and they may turn inwards instead of outwards.

When a baby sucks at its mother's breast, a hormone from her pituitary allows milk to flow out of the ducts through microscopic holes in the nipple.

The area around the nipple is called the areola. It varies from pink to dark brown in shade, becoming darker during pregnancy.

The tiny lumps in the areola are glands. During breast-feeding, these produce a fatty substance which helps to protect the nipples.

Stray hairs often grow in the areola. You can pluck them out or cut them off if you want.

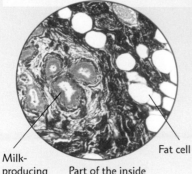

Milk-producing area

Part of the inside of a breast

Fat cell

As the milk-collecting ducts enlarge at puberty, fat is formed to provide a protective cushion for them. It is the amount of fat in your breasts which determines their size.

The ducts are separated from each other by elastic fibres. These tend to stretch as you get older, which makes the breasts begin to droop.

Bras

It is up to you when you start to wear a bra. There is no medical reason to wear one, but some girls feel less self-conscious if they do, and most women find it more comfortable for exercising or sport.

The weight of large breasts can sometimes stretch the fibres in them prematurely so that the breasts start to droop; so if you have large breasts it may be a good idea to wear a bra most of the time.

Measuring up

To buy a bra, you need to have a rough idea of your chest measurement and cup size. You can usually be measured in a good store's underwear department; a trained measurer will probably be able to measure you without you even having to take your top off, so long as the top is fairly thin. If you prefer, you can measure yourself at home by following the instructions given below.

1 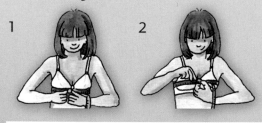 2

1. To find out your chest size, measure tightly around your ribcage just under your breasts and add 12cm (5in) to the measurement, e.g:
68cm (27in) + 12cm (5in) = 80cm (32in).

2. To find out your cup size, measure around the fullest part of your breasts, across the nipples. If this is the same as the measurement above, you are an AA cup; if there is a 10-15mm (½in) difference, you are an A cup; a 2.5cm (1in) difference means you are a B cup; a 5cm (2in) difference makes you a C, and a 7.5cm (3in) difference a D.

Buying a bra

For a bra to be comfortable and give you a good shape, it needs to fit you exactly right. If it is too big, it will wrinkle and move around, and may even ride up. If it is too small, not only will it feel tight but you will bulge out of it.

For normal, everyday wear, a full-cup bra in soft, stretchy material is usually the most comfortable. Shorten or lengthen the bra straps to fit, and fasten in whichever position at the back fits you best.

Don't be surprised if the bra size you think you are doesn't fit. All makes and styles of bra fit differently and the sizing is only a guide. Just keep trying on lots of different makes and styles until you find one that fits you well. Then put on your top so you can see what you will look like with your clothes on. Some bras change your natural shape much more than others.

Female sex organs

Girls are often unaware of the changes in their sex organs, because most of them are inside their body. This page tells you about the female sex organs which are outside the body. External sex organs are called genitals. Girls' genitals are less obvious than boys'.

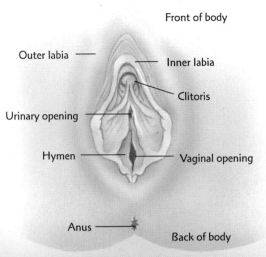

Front of body
Outer labia
Inner labia
Clitoris
Urinary opening
Hymen
Vaginal opening
Anus
Back of body

Vulva: the female genitals are called the vulva. The only way you can really see your vulva is to use a mirror.

Don't worry if yours looks different from the one in this picture. Genitals vary from person to person just like any other part of the body.

Outer labia: these are two thick folds of skin or "lips". They are made of fat and have pubic hair on them. They are normally closed over the inner parts of the vulva, protecting them.

Inner labia: these are thinner than the outer labia and hairless. As you grow up, they become more sensitive to touch. A lubricating fluid is made by glands in the labia. The left and right labia are rarely the same size, and sometimes they stick out from between the outer labia.

Clitoris: this is the most sensitive part of the female body. It is the equivalent of the male's penis, although it is only about the size of a pea. The exact size varies from woman to woman and is not related to sensitivity. Only the tip of the clitoris is visible. This has a fold of skin or "hood" over it, formed by the inner labia meeting at the front of the vulva.

Urinary opening: this is the opening of the urethra, which is the tube leading from your bladder to the outside of your body. It is where your urine comes out.

Vaginal opening: this is the opening to the vagina, which is a tube leading to your internal sex organs. A small amount of cleansing and moisturising fluid leaks out from it. It is where the blood comes out when you have a period (see page 20), where the penis fits during sex (see page 30) and where babies leave the body when they are born. Although the opening is very small, it stretches easily.

Hymen: this is a thin layer of skin over the vaginal opening. It breaks down as your vagina grows and stretches at puberty, or may have broken earlier if you do a lot of sport. If yours still seems intact, there will still be enough tiny holes in it for period blood to get out.

Anus: this is the hole at the end of your digestive tract where solid waste (faeces) leaves your body when you go to the toilet.

Female sex organs inside the body

Like the rest of the body, the internal female sex organs grow a lot at puberty. The picture on the right shows how they look.

The sex organs are seen here from the front and most of them are drawn so that you can see inside them.

Ovaries: a female has two ovaries. They are low down in her abdomen, one on each side, and are attached to the outside of the uterus (womb) by connecting fibres. Fully developed ovaries are about the shape and size of shelled walnuts.

When a girl is born, she already has hundreds of thousands of ova (egg cells) stored in her ovaries. At puberty, the hormones FSH and LH, produced by the pituitary, make the ova begin to mature and be released from the ovaries. Usually, one ovum is released each month, from alternate ovaries. This is called ovulation. The process continues until the age of about 50. The time when it stops is called the menopause.

Where are the internal sex organs?

The two pictures below show the position of the female sex organs in the abdomen. The picture on the left shows how the organs (especially the uterus) are protected by the bones of the pelvis.

This picture is a sideways view, so that you can see where the sex organs are positioned in relation to the bladder and rectum (back passage) and how they connect up with the external sex organs.

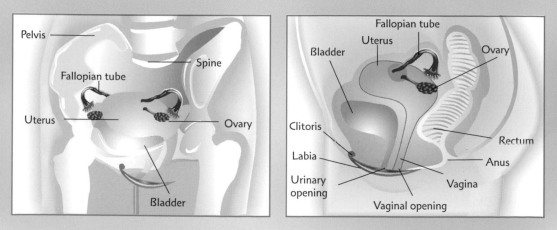

Pelvis — Spine — Fallopian tube — Uterus — Ovary — Bladder

Fallopian tube — Uterus — Bladder — Ovary — Clitoris — Labia — Urinary opening — Vaginal opening — Vagina — Anus — Rectum

Fallopian tubes: the fallopian, or uterine, tubes are about 12cm (4¾in) long and the thickness of a pencil. The hollow part is only the width of the lead of a pencil.

When an ovum is released from an ovary, the fringed end of the nearest fallopian tube swoops down and draws it into the tube.

The muscular walls of the tube and tiny hairs inside it then move the ovum along towards the uterus.

It is while an ovum is in the tube that a woman may become pregnant if she has sex. A sperm cell (from the man's body) may fertilize the ovum. You can find out more about this on page 32.

Uterus: the ovum passes from the fallopian tube into the cavity of the uterus. The uterus is normally about the shape and size of a pear turned upside down. It has thick muscular walls and many blood vessels in its inner lining. The lining changes in response to changes in the levels of the sex hormones, oestrogen and progesterone, produced by the ovaries. Every month, from puberty to the menopause, the lining of the uterus thickens in preparation for a fertilized ovum to embed itself in it and start developing into a baby.

When fertilization does not take place, the ovum disintegrates, the lining of the uterus breaks down and you have a period. The lining passes out of your vagina along with blood. You can find out more about periods on pages 20-25.

Cervix: this is known as the "neck of the womb". It is a narrow passageway, or "canal", about 2mm (⅛in) wide, which connects the uterus and vagina. When a woman gives birth, the canal gets much wider to let the baby pass through.

Vagina: this is a muscular tube, about 10cm (4in) long, connecting the uterus with the outside of the body. Normally, the walls of the vagina are quite close together but they are arranged in folds rather like a concertina. This means they can stretch enormously and easily, enough to let a baby be born. Glands in the lining of the vagina produce a cleansing and lubricating fluid.

Periods

Starting to have periods is probably the single most important change of puberty for girls. Below you can see how periods happen because the lining of the uterus breaks down and causes a small amount of bleeding from the vagina. This may sound scary but, if you are prepared for it, it is nothing at all to worry about. The blood trickles out gradually over a few days and good-quality tampons or sanitary towels can easily absorb the flow.

When do periods start?

Periods can start any time between the ages of eight and 17, but the most usual time is about 2½ years after your breasts have begun to develop. There is nothing you can do to make your periods start or to delay them starting once they are ready to.

Hormones and periods

Here you can see how the period cycle is controlled by hormones. The cycle given here is an average one lasting 28 days. Yours may be different.

Day 1
The period starts. At the same time, the hormone FSH from the pituitary is making an ovum mature in a tiny sac or "follicle" in one of the ovaries. (You can see the ovum in its follicle in the photograph opposite.)

Day 5
The period is over. The ovum continues to mature and the follicle moves towards the surface of the ovary. The follicle is producing the hormone oestrogen. This makes the lining of the uterus start to thicken again.

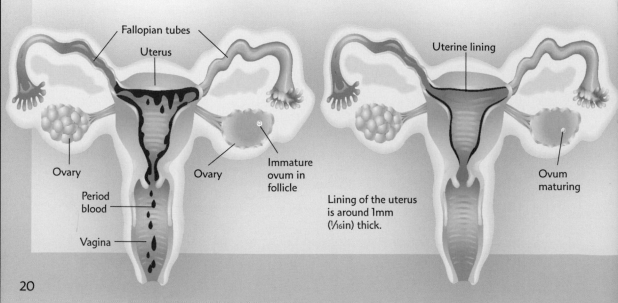

Fallopian tubes

Uterus

Ovary

Period blood

Vagina

Immature ovum in follicle

Ovary

Uterine lining

Lining of the uterus is around 1mm (⅟₁₆in) thick.

Ovum maturing

How often, how long?

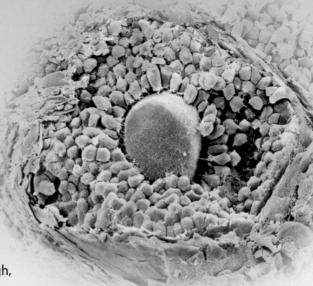

A woman has a period about every four weeks (28 days). The cycle can vary, though, from about 20 days to 35 from woman to woman, and even in the same woman from month to month. A period lasts from two to about eight days, but the average is five.

This is an enlarged photograph of an ovum in an ovary. The ovum would really be only about the size of a full stop. The blue blobs are cells that nourish the ovum while it develops.

Day 14

The pituitary stops producing FSH and produces LH instead. This makes the now mature ovum burst out of its follicle, leave the ovary (ovulation) and enter the fallopian tube. The empty follicle, known as the "yellow body", starts to produce the second female sex hormone, progesterone. Progesterone makes the thickening lining of the uterus soft and spongy so that if the ovum is fertilized, it can embed itself.

Day 21

The ovum has been in the uterus for a few days now. If it has not been fertilized, both it and the yellow body start to disintegrate and the levels of oestrogen and progesterone fall. The lining of the uterus starts to disintegrate and come away from the walls of the uterus. Some of the blood vessels kink and tear in the process. On day 1, the next period starts and the cycle begins again.

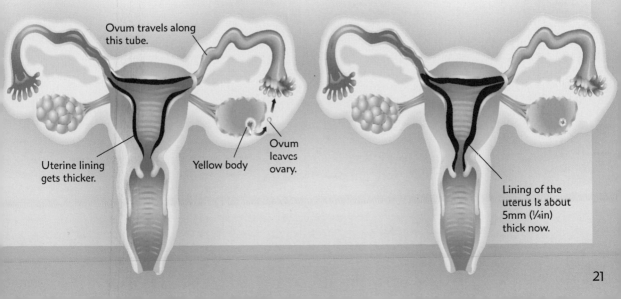

Ovum travels along this tube.

Uterine lining gets thicker.

Yellow body

Ovum leaves ovary.

Lining of the uterus Is about 5mm (¼in) thick now.

How much blood?

You appear to lose only blood when you have a period but the flow really consists of cells from the lining of the uterus, which are simply stained with blood and mixed with a sticky fluid from the cervix. The blood comes from small blood vessels in the uterus which tear as the lining comes away from the walls. On average, you lose 2-4 tablespoons of blood per period.

What to wear

You have a choice of using either sanitary towels (pads) or tampons to absorb period blood. Towels soak it up as it leaves your body from the vaginal opening, whereas tampons fit right inside the vagina and catch it before it leaves your body.

Both towels and tampons are fairly expensive. You may see adverts in magazines offering free samples. It is worth sending off for these, as you may need to try quite a few different types and makes before you find what suits you best.

Towels

Towels come in different sizes (from normal to extra long for example), so you can choose one to fit the shape of your body. They also come in different thicknesses (from ultra thin to ultra absorbent), so you can also choose one to suit the heaviness of your period.

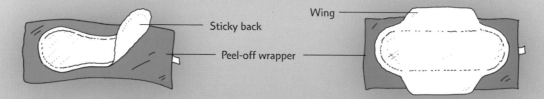

Sticky back

Peel-off wrapper

Wing

Most towels have a sticky stripe on the back which you press to your pants to hold the towel in place. These are comfortable, but you may take a while to get used to sticking them in exactly the right position.

Some towels have side flaps or "wings", as well as a sticky stripe on the back. The flaps stick to the underside of your pants to hold the towel in place extra firmly. They also make the towels more absorbent.

Changing towels

It is best to change your towel every few hours, even if your flow is not heavy. Period blood is perfectly clean, but once it's outside your body it meets bacteria from the air and this can cause a smell or even an infection.

Flushing towels down the toilet blocks the pipes and is bad for the environment. Instead, put them in an old plastic bag and throw them in the waste bin. You can always carry a bag with you when you go out, and bins are often provided in public toilets. You can put individually wrapped towels back in their wrapper to thow away.

Tampons

Many women prefer tampons to towels. Once a tampon is in the right position in your vagina, you can't feel it at all. You don't need to worry about people seeing the shape of a towel through tight clothes, or be anxious about any smell. You can have a bath or go swimming.

Tampons come in different sizes (from mini to super-plus-extra, for example). The size you need depends on how heavy your period is, rather than on the size of your body. There are two kinds of tampons.

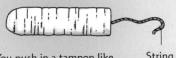

You push in a tampon like this with your finger.

String for pulling out.

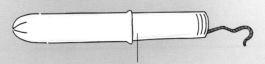

Some tampons come with applicators. When you push this end of the applicator, the tampon comes out the other end.

Changing tampons

It isn't as easy to tell when a tampon needs to be changed as it is a towel, though you can sometimes feel a bubbling sensation just before the tampon starts to leak and the string may become bloodstained. You should change tampons every four hours or sooner anyway, and not leave one in for longer than eight hours overnight. If you are going to sleep for longer, it is best to wear a towel. If you leave tampons in too long, bacteria in the vagina may cause infection.

Tampons will usually flush down the toilet but it is better for the environment if you dispose of them in the same way as towels (see opposite page).

Inserting a tampon

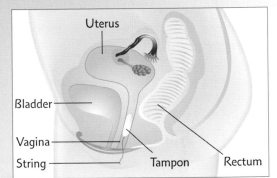

Some girls don't want to try tampons when they first start their periods, but there is no medical reason not to, if you feel like it. Start with a small size; you can always go on to bigger ones if they can't cope with your flow.

Tampons come with instructions and you should read and follow these very carefully. The best time to try inserting a tampon for the first time is when your period is heaviest. Wash your hands before unwrapping a tampon to guard against infection and if you drop one on the floor, don't use it. If you can't get a tampon in, it may mean that your hymen is still fairly intact, but is more likely to mean that you haven't been able to relax enough. Just try again another time.

Toxic shock syndrome

This is a very rare but serious illness; half the cases occur in young women using tampons. Read your tampon leaflet to find out about the symptoms and what to do if you develop them.

To help reduce your risk of suffering from toxic shock, use the smallest size of tampons you can and change them frequently; wear towels some of the time, especially at night and when your flow is very light; never wear a tampon when you are not having a period; and store tampons away from heat and moisture.

Being prepared

Most people first notice a period has started when they go to the toilet. As your periods may be irregular at first, it can be a good idea always to have a towel or tampon with you just in case one starts. Individually wrapped towels are useful for carrying around.

Some women wear a pant-liner if they are expecting a period to start. These are like very small, thin sanitary towels. You can even buy thong-shaped liners although these would not cope with much blood.

Wrapped pant-liner

Thong-shaped pant-liner

If you get caught out, towels and tampons are sold from coin machines in toilets. If you are at school, a teacher or someone in the school office can help you. In a real emergency, tissues, paper towels or a wad of toilet paper is better than nothing at all.

Feeling embarrassed

At first, you may feel as though everyone can tell you are having a period just by looking at you. They can't. Even so, you may feel less self-conscious if you wear loose-fitting trousers, or dark-coloured ones just in case of a leak.

If you do leak, try tying your jumper round your waist to hide it, or turn your skirt round so people will think you've spilled something down your front.

Baths and swimming

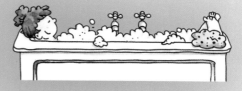

It is fine to have a bath when you are having a period; the blood doesn't flow as fast while you are in water. Just put a wad of toilet paper between your legs when you get out, so you don't get blood on your bath towel. For more about washing your genital area, see page 49.

If you feel like going swimming, there is no reason not to, but you will need to wear a tampon.

Myths about periods

Over the centuries, there have been many myths about periods. Most date from the time when the cause of them was not understood. Some superstitions survived until quite recently, such as you shouldn't wash your hair when you have a period, or eat ice cream. In reality, a woman can do everything she normally does, unless she has religious reasons not to.

Periods and pregnancy

Women don't have periods when they are pregnant. If someone's period doesn't come at the expected time and she has had sex since her last period, she may well be pregnant and would need to have a pregnancy test to find out.

Coping with periods

Having periods is a normal, healthy process, not an illness, and many women have no problems at all with them. On the other hand, the female hormone cycle is very complex. A male's sex hormone levels stay more or less the same from day to day.

A female's are changing every day over the course of her cycle. The hormones are carried in your bloodstream, so they can affect other parts of your body besides your sex organs. Some women don't feel quite like their normal selves before or during their period.

Painful periods

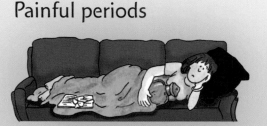

Quite a lot of women get an ache or cramp-like pains in their lower abdomen at the start of a period. Doctors think this is caused by hormones making the muscles of the uterus contract (get smaller).

If the pain is only slight, exercise can help. If it is very bad, you may need to take a painkiller and lie down with a hot water bottle. If you get really bad period pains every month, so that you can't do what you would normally do (go to school, play sport, enjoy weekends), then go to the doctor about it.

Heavy periods

Usually, a period starts off fairly slowly, then gets heavier for a couple of days, then eases off towards the end. Some women only ever have a light flow, while others have a heavier one for the whole period. Both can be perfectly normal.

If someone has really heavy periods, she may become anaemic (symptoms are being very tired, pale and breathless). Go to the doctor's if you regularly soak more than six of the largest-size towels or tampons per day for more than two days, or if every period goes on for more than seven days.

PMS

Some women suffer from premenstrual syndrome (PMS) for a few days before a period. PMS, also known as premenstrual tension (PMT), is probably caused by changing hormone levels. Symptoms include sore, swollen breasts, a bloated, heavy feeling especially in the abdomen, headaches, spots, and feeling clumsy, tired, irritable or depressed. There is no proven medical remedy but a healthy diet may help (see pages 38-41); so might eating little but often throughout the day. Exercise and extra sleep can also make you feel better.

Irregular periods

These are not necessarily a problem. It is quite usual for periods to be irregular for the first year or two. This is because your hormones are not yet in a regular rhythm. You may even find that a few months pass between periods. Other reasons for periods becoming irregular include being ill, losing a lot of weight, feeling upset, worried or stressed, and even just changing your normal routine.

Crystals of the female sex hormone, progesterone, dyed and magnified.

Male sex organs

It is easy for a boy to tell when his sex organs are developing because they increase visibly in size. The testicles start to get bigger and the penis follows about a year later. The picture below shows the male sex organs from the front. They are drawn so you can see the different parts.

Testicles: the male's testicles are the equivalent of the female's ovaries. They produce male sex cells (sperm) and the male sex hormone, testosterone. Testicles are about the size of small plums. The left one usually hangs lower than the right.

From puberty on, sperm are being formed all the time in tiny tubes inside the testicles.

It takes over two months for a sperm to be formed. Several million complete the process every day. Unlike the ovaries, the testicles don't stop producing sex cells in middle age. Production continues, though at a lower level, right into old age. This means men can go on having children for longer than women can.

Scrotum: the testicles are contained in a loose pouch of wrinkled skin called the scrotum. They are outside the abdomen, as sperm are only produced at a temperature around 2°C (4°F) lower than normal internal body temperature. When your testicles are exposed to cold, the skin of your scrotum shrinks, drawing them closer to your body for warmth.

Epididymis: the epididymis is a coiled tube which lies over the back of each testicle. Each tube would be 6m (20ft) long if it was uncoiled. The sperm move from the testicles into the epididymis, where they mature for about two weeks.

Sperm ducts: these are two tubes, about 40cm (16in) long, which lead from the epididymis up into the pelvis. There, they join into the urethra as it leaves the bladder. The ducts are muscular and about the thickness of string. The sperm travel along the ducts from the epididymis towards the penis.

Seminal vesicles: these are glands. They produce a nourishing fluid which helps to give the sperm energy.

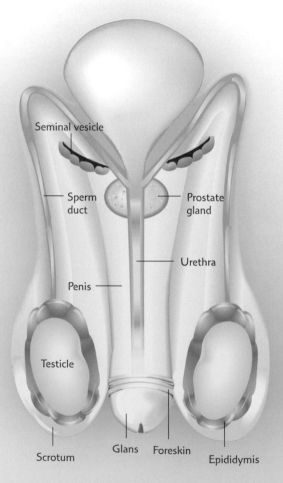

Seminal vesicle

Sperm duct

Prostate gland

Urethra

Penis

Testicle

Scrotum   Glans   Foreskin   Epididymis

The male sex organs, drawn so you can see inside.

Prostate gland: this is about the size of a walnut and produces a fluid which helps the sperm to move.

Urethra: this is longer in males than females and has two functions. One is to carry urine to the outside of the body. During sexual excitement it carries semen, which is the mixture of sperm and the fluids produced by the seminal vesicles and the prostate gland.

Penis: usually the penis is fairly small and soft. During sexual excitement, more blood flows into it than usual, and less flows out, so it becomes larger and harder and stands away from the body (an erection). This means it can fit inside the female's vagina. Sperm can be deposited in the vagina so that a baby can be made.

Glans: this is the name for the tip of the penis, which is the most sensitive part.

Foreskin: this is the fold of skin which covers the glans of the penis. Glands under the foreskin produce a white, creamy substance called smegma. This helps the skin to slide back smoothly over the glans.

Position of the sex organs

This picture shows the male sex organs viewed from the right.

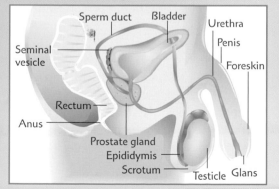

Circumcision

In some religions, for example the Jewish and Muslim ones, it is the custom to cut away a boy's foreskin surgically. This is called circumcision.

In some countries, such as the US, the operation is routinely performed because it is believed to be more hygienic. When the foreskin is intact, smegma can collect beneath it, causing a smell or occasionally an infection. However, if you roll back your foreskin and wash gently underneath it every day, you can avoid this problem.

Penis size

The size of unerect penises varies from male to male and has no relation to body size. Some boys worry about having a small penis. In fact, small penises generally increase their size a lot more than large ones when they become erect, so that apparent differences become much less. The average length of an erect penis is between 12.5 and 15.25cm (5 and 6in). In any case, most females are less interested in size than in how sensitively their partner makes love with them.

Sex

As the levels of your sex hormones increase and your sex organs mature, you become more aware of sexual feelings. This may start with an increased awareness of your own body and emotions, which develops to include an interest in the opposite sex. At first, this may take the form of dreams and fantasies. Later, it becomes a desire for physical contact and ultimately for sex.

In many countries, sexual intercourse (see page 30) is illegal under a certain age, known as the "age of consent" – 16 in Britain, for example. This doesn't mean that once you reach the age of consent, you have to have sex. You shouldn't let anyone pressure you into it before you feel completely ready and have considered all the consequences, including pregnancy and disease.

Embarrassing erections

Most boys are embarrassed by having erections at inconvenient moments during puberty. Most erections are triggered by a sexual thought, for example when you see someone you fancy. Some happen when your genitals are accidentally stimulated, for example by the vibrations of a moving train. The best way to make the erections subside is to concentrate very hard on thinking about something else.

It is very common for males to wake up with an erection in the morning. This is due to dreaming, but not necessarily about sex.

Fantasies

It is common to fantasize during puberty. Some people like to fantasize about someone they know, or about famous people, such as pop singers or film stars. Other people make up imaginary characters. You may be surprised or troubled at the form some of your fantasies take. Don't worry: fantasies give you the opportunity to imagine doing things that might be unacceptable if you were to do them in real life.

Wet dreams

Wet dreams are common in boys during puberty. While you are asleep, you have an erection and semen squirts (ejaculates) out of your penis. This happens while you are dreaming, though not necessarily about sex. It is nothing to worry about: your body is just getting used to its new way of working.

If you feel embarrassed about staining the sheets, you can sponge the stain out with soap and cold water, or keep tissues or toilet paper near the bed for mopping up.

Kissing, touching and stroking

1. Most people have quite a lot of physical contact of a nonsexual kind with their family and close friends, which may involve touching and kissing.

2. The areas of the body that are the most sexually sensitive are called the erogenous zones. These include the genitals, lips, breasts and buttocks, but ear lobes, feet and many other areas are sensitive in different people.

3. Snogging is a word used to describe sexual kissing, touching and stroking. It often involves deep kissing on the lips, sometimes called "French kissing", when one or both partners put their tongue in the other's mouth.

Sexual contact often involves touching or stroking areas of another person's body that you wouldn't normally touch. The erogenous zones, such as the breasts or genitals, tend to be touched most.

Sexual kissing and touching usually create a feeling of intense pleasure in both partners and may lead to a desire for intercourse. Snogging doesn't have to end in sex, though: it can be a pleasurable end in itself.

Masturbation

Masturbation means handling the genitals to give sexual pleasure, either to yourself or to someone else.

Males generally masturbate by rubbing their penis rhythmically up and down in their hand, while females generally stroke the area around the clitoris rhythmically with their fingers.

There used to be lots of myths about the bad effects of masturbation, for example it could make you blind. In fact, masturbation only becomes unhealthy if someone wants to do it all the time.

Masturbation may lead to an orgasm, which is the climax of sexual excitement both for males and females. It is often called "coming". An orgasm is a series of brief muscular spasms (contractions) in the sex organs. These are felt as a throbbing or pulsating sensation, which can spread through the whole body, and cause a feeling of intense pleasure followed by a feeling of relaxation.

In males, semen is ejaculated out of the penis by the muscular contractions of orgasm (see page 30).

Sexual intercourse

1. Strictly speaking, sexual intercourse begins when a male's penis enters a female's vagina, and ends when it is withdrawn. However, intercourse, or "making love", almost always begins with a period of kissing, touching and stroking which is known as foreplay.

2. Once the penis is inside the vagina, one or both partners moves their pelvis, so that it slides in and out repeatedly. This creates a sensation of pleasure. This stage can last from less than a minute to several minutes, with changes of rhythm and rest periods.

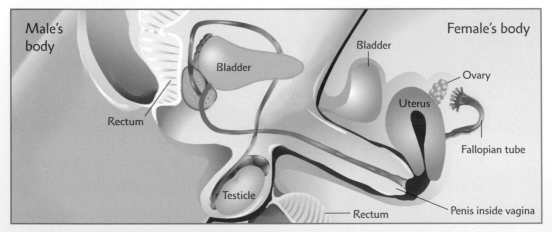

Male's body — Bladder — Rectum — Testicle

Female's body — Bladder — Ovary — Uterus — Fallopian tube — Rectum — Penis inside vagina

3. Eventually, because of the stimulation to the penis and the clitoris, orgasm usually takes place. One partner may reach orgasm before the other, or a couple may have their orgasms at the same time.

Orgasm may not happen every time, especially in females. The semen that is ejaculated out of the penis when the male has an orgasm can lead to the woman becoming pregnant.

Changes in the body

Sexual excitement brings about a whole range of changes in the body.

In women's bodies, glands in the vagina produce a lubricating fluid, so that the penis can enter it more easily. The woman's breasts may get larger and the nipples become erect.

In men's bodies, the penis becomes larger and harder, and points upwards at an angle away from the body (an erection), so it can fit into the vagina. The testicles swell and are drawn closer to the body.

In both sexes, muscles all over the body become firmer, the heart beats faster, blood pressure rises and breathing becomes faster and shallow. The face may become flushed.

Ejaculation

The semen ejaculated from the penis at orgasm is a mixture of sperm (male sex cells) and fluids produced by the seminal vesicles and prostate gland (see pages 26 and 27).

On average, only a teaspoonful of semen comes out of the penis with each ejaculation, but this contains hundreds of millions of sperm.

The muscular contractions of orgasm squeeze the sperm from their storage place near the testicles, through the sperm ducts to the urethra, which leads from the bladder through the length of the penis. Muscles around the base of the bladder act as a valve and ensure that urine can't pass down the urethra at the same time as semen.

Sex and emotions

Sex is not just about physical sensations; it usually involves very strong emotions as well. How people feel about it usually depends a great deal on how emotionally involved they are with their partner and on how much they trust them. Problems with sex often have emotional causes. Anxiety, shyness, fear and unhappiness can all have physical effects on the body. If a couple can talk to each other about any problems, this is the best way towards solving them.

One of the few occasions when a problem with sex is likely to be purely physical is if a woman experiences slight pain and bleeding when the penis pierces the hymen (see page 17) the first time she has intercourse.

Sex and pregnancy

There is always a chance that sexual intercourse could make a woman or girl pregnant, unless special precautions are taken to prevent a baby from starting. These precautions are known as contraception (meaning "against conception"). You can find out about contraception on pages 32-35.

The right to say "no"

Sex can make people feel good but it can also make them feel very bad, if they have it when they don't really want to or aren't completely ready to, or without taking precautions against pregnancy or sexually transmitted infections.

Sometimes people try to persuade or even force someone else into having sexual contact with them. They don't have the right to do this. If someone touches you, or talks to you, in a way that makes you feel uncomfortable, tell them to stop. If they persist, tell an adult you trust about their behaviour. Everyone has the right to say "no".

Homosexuality

Being homosexual, or gay, means being sexually attracted only, or mainly, to people of your own sex. Female homosexuals are usually known as lesbians. (People who are attracted only, or mainly, to the opposite sex are heterosexual, or straight.) Some people are bisexual, which means they can be attracted to both sexes. A person's sexuality can fluctuate over the course of their lifetime.

It is common, and quite normal, to experience strong feelings for someone of the same sex, especially during puberty. Such feelings at puberty will often, though not always, be followed by strong attraction to the opposite sex.

No one really knows why some people are attracted to their own sex, while others are not. It can take a long time for people to "come out" and tell others that they are gay. This is usually because some heterosexuals are critical of homosexuals, although such prejudice is less common than it used to be.

Sex and the Internet

Be very wary of anyone you meet on the Internet. Paedophiles (adults who are sexually attracted to children) can be very clever at pretending to be young and friendly, in the hope of luring you to meet them. Never tell anyone online your full name, telephone number, or home or school address, and ask your parent's or guardian's permission before giving your e-mail address.

Contraception

The process of becoming pregnant after having sex is called conception. There are various measures a couple can take to prevent pregnancy happening. This is called contraception (against conception).

Some methods of contraception are more effective than others. In many countries they are provided free and in confidence through family doctors or at family planning or sexual health clinics.

Conception

When a male ejaculates semen inside a female's vagina during intercourse, hundreds of millions of sperm cells are deposited close to the cervix. From there, sperm swim up through the uterus and into the fallopian tubes. Only about a thousand sperm get as far as the tubes before they die. If there is an ovum in one of the tubes, the sperm cluster around it and one sperm may join with it. This moment is called fertilization: the start of conception. Together, the ovum and sperm make one new cell. This grows and develops into a baby in the female's uterus.

Fallopian tubes
Sperm
Ovum
Ovary
Ovary
Uterus
Cervix
Sperm deposited here.
Penis

One sperm joins with ovum.
Ovum and sperm enlarged

Combined pill or patch

These are two of the most effective methods of contraception. The woman takes pills or wears a patch on her skin. The pills and patches contain oestrogen and progestogen (similar to progesterone). They work mainly by lowering the output of the hormones FSH and LH from the woman's pituitary so that no ova mature in her ovaries and ovulation cannot take place.

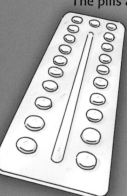

The pills and patches must be prescribed by a doctor or nurse and the woman has regular checkups to make sure she is not suffering from side effects. At first these can include headaches, sore breasts and weight changes. In very rare cases, a woman may develop a more serious complaint such as a thrombosis (blood clot). One good side effect of the pill and patch is that periods become lighter, more regular and more pain-free. For this reason they are sometimes specially prescribed for women who have problems with their periods.

Progestogen-only pill (POP)

This is only very slightly less effective than the combined pill or patch. The pills contain progestogen only and work mainly by thickening a fluid which is produced by the woman's cervix so that sperm find it too difficult to swim through it.

The pills also ensure that if an ovum is fertilized, it cannot embed itself. The progestogen-only pill is prescribed by a doctor or nurse and the woman has regular checkups. Side effects can include irregular periods, spots and sore breasts.

Condoms

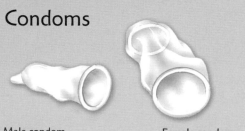

Male condom   Female condom

A male condom is a thin sheath which is put onto the man's erect penis before intercourse. When he ejaculates, the semen is caught in the end of the sheath. He has to remove his penis very carefully from the vagina soon after ejaculating, or the sheath may slip off as his penis shrinks back to normal size.

A female condom is a sheath which is put into the vagina to line it and catch the semen during intercourse. The couple have to be careful that the open end of the condom stays outside the vagina and that the penis goes into the condom and not between the condom and the vagina.

Condoms are free from family planning and sexual health clinics. They are on sale in chemists', supermarkets and often from coin machines in toilets.

Condoms are the only method of contraception which helps to give some protection against sexually transmitted infections, including HIV (see pages 36-37).

Diaphragms and caps

Diaphragm

Spermicide

Diaphragms and caps are made of soft rubber or silicone. They fit over the cervix and help prevent sperm from entering the uterus. To be effective, they must be smeared with "spermicide". This is a cream or jelly containing chemicals which help to kill sperm. (Spermicides are not effective when used on their own.)

The woman has to be measured for a diaphragm or cap by a doctor or nurse. She then inserts it herself before having intercourse and must leave it in place for several hours afterwards, for the spermicide to act. Neither she nor the man can feel the diaphragm or cap during intercourse if it has been inserted properly.

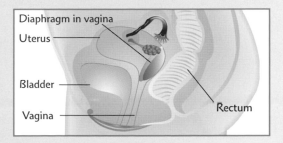

Diaphragm in vagina

Uterus

Bladder

Vagina

Rectum

IUD and IUS

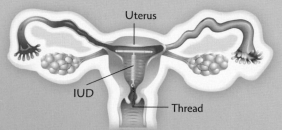

Uterus

IUD

Thread

These are two similar methods. An IUD (intra-uterine device), which used to be called a coil, is made of plastic and copper; an IUS (intra-uterine system) is a plastic device containing progestogen. They are put into a woman's uterus and work mainly by preventing sperm from meeting an ovum.

The IUD or IUS is inserted by a doctor or nurse, through the woman's vagina, and can then be kept in place for several years, without her being aware of it. She checks regularly that it has not fallen out by feeling for a thread left hanging down into the top of her vagina.

IUDs can cause heavy or painful periods. With an IUS, periods become much lighter but there is a risk of spots and sore breasts at first.

Natural methods

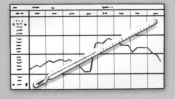

Temperature graph

An ovum lives for only about 24 hours after ovulation. Sperm can live inside a woman's body for up to seven days. This means that if a couple do not have intercourse from seven days before ovulation to one day after, conception should not take place. However, the trouble is that it is extremely difficult to predict ovulation. Couples try to work it out using a combination of three methods: from the dates of the woman's last period; by noting fluctuations in her temperature during her cycle; and by examining a fluid produced by the cervix for changes in its appearance. They need the help of a qualified teacher to learn how to do this successfully. It is possible to buy kits which monitor ovulation more accurately by measuring hormone levels, but these are expensive.

Implants and injections

Implant, shown actual size

Injection

These are effective, long-term methods of contraception. An implant is a small, soft tube which is inserted by a doctor or nurse under the skin of a woman's upper arm. The implant gradually releases progestogen into the woman's body and this prevents an egg and sperm meeting. An implant works for up to three years and the woman has regular checkups during this period.

The implant can be removed if necessary.

A contraceptive injection slowly releases progestogen into the woman's body to prevent ovulation. One injection lasts for two or three months. This means that any side effects do too.

The side effects of both implants and injections include changes in the woman's periods.

Non-methods of contraception

Here are a few myths about contraception. *"The woman cannot become pregnant if ..."*

1... the man withdraws his penis from the vagina before he ejaculates." This is untrue because sperm leak out of the penis before ejaculation. If the man ejaculates near the vagina after withdrawal, sperm may get into it.

2... she lies on top of the man during intercourse or if the couple both stand up." Gravity may mean that fewer sperm swim up into the uterus but very many still will.

3... she is having a period." Sperm can swim through blood; they live for up to seven days, and an ovum may be released into a fallopian tube early in the woman's cycle.

4... she goes to the toilet immediately after intercourse." The sperm will not be flushed out of her body because the vagina and urethra are totally separate.

5... it is the first time she has had intercourse or she has only just started having periods." It is true that some girls start having periods before they are ovulating properly but, as a rule, anyone who has started her periods, or is about to have her first period, may become pregnant.

6... she does not have an orgasm." Contractions of the uterus during orgasm may help to suck the sperm in but they also enter very easily without them.

Failure rate

You can see how reliable different methods of contraception are below. The figures show how many women in 100 get pregnant using that method for a year.

Combined pill or patch	almost 0%
Progestogen-only pill	1%
Male condom	2%
Female condom	5%
Diaphragm and cap	4-10%
IUD	1-2%
IUS	almost 0%
Implant	almost 0%
Injection	almost 0%
Natural methods	2-15%
No contraception	80-90%

Emergency contraception

If a couple forget to use contraception or, say, a condom splits, there are two methods of emergency contraception. One is for the woman to take two doses of "the morning after pill"; despite its name, if this method is started within three days (72 hours) after intercourse, it usually prevents ovulation, or stops a fertilized ovum from embedding in the uterus. The pills are bought at chemists' or provided free by doctors or clinics. They are not as effective as using other methods of contraception regularly. The other emergency method is for the woman to have an IUD inserted within five days after intercourse.

Abortion

This is not a method of contraception but a way of ending a pregnancy once it has begun. Another word for abortion is termination. In early pregnancy, the woman takes pills to make the contents of the uterus pass out of her vagina like a very heavy period. Later in pregnancy, she has an operation to suck or scrape out the contents.

The risks of abortion include infection.

In some countries abortion is illegal. In others it is legal under certain conditions. In Britain, for example, it is legal up to the 24th week of pregnancy. Two doctors have to agree that the pregnancy would harm the mother's physical or mental health, or that the baby might be born disabled.

Sexually transmitted infections

Sexually transmitted infections (STIs) are also known as sexually transmitted diseases (STDs), venereal diseases (VDs) or genito-urinary diseases. There are many different types. Some individual infections are listed in the glossary.

What are STIs?

STIs are infections in the sex organs caused by microbes (microscopic creatures) such as viruses or bacteria. They are passed from one person to another during sexual contact.

What are the symptoms?

The first symptoms of many STIs are similar. They can include itching or soreness of the genitals or anus; a sore, blister, lump or rash in that area; a discharge; and pain when going to the toilet. Sometimes people can have an STI and infect a partner without knowing it, because they have no symptoms.

How are STIs passed on?

Different STIs are passed on by different kinds of sexual contact: vaginal or anal intercourse, oral sex (see the glossary), or genital skin contact. Some STIs can be caught when an infected person's blood gets into another person's body. For this reason, drug users who share injecting equipment are at risk, and the needles used for body piercing, tattooing and acupuncture must always be sterilized or brand-new. You can't catch a serious STI by kissing on the lips. Cold sores are often passed on this way though.

What is the treatment?

Many STIs can be cured if they are treated early enough. One exception is HIV (see opposite page). Infections caused by bacteria can be treated with antibiotics. Viral infections can't be cured but the symptoms can often be treated effectively. In many countries (including Britain), people worried they may have an STI can have a free and confidential checkup at their doctor's, or the STI or GUM clinic of their local hospital. Even STIs which are not yet showing symptoms can be diagnosed by tests. Left untreated, STIs can lead to serious long-term health problems.

Chlamydia

Chlamydia is a very common and serious STI. It may cause no obvious symptoms but can scar a woman's fallopian tubes, leading to long-term pain and leaving her infertile (unable to have children). Tests can diagnose it, even if it is symptomless. It is caused by bacteria, and so can be treated with antibiotics.

How can STIs be avoided?

The fewer sexual partners a person has, the less risk they have of coming into contact with someone who has an STI. Condoms help to protect against diseases passed on through sexual intercourse. Some new partners have a checkup at the doctor's or a clinic before they start having sex. It is unwise to share razors or toothbrushes (because many people's gums bleed when they clean their teeth).

Chlamydia bacteria, magnified thousands of times.

HIV

HIV stands for human immunodeficiency virus. It is the most serious of the STIs because it is incurable and many sufferers eventually die.

What does HIV do?

When someone catches any virus, white blood cells in their body produce antibodies which attack and kill the virus. HIV can actually destroy these white blood cells so the person is unable to fight off infections. Someone with HIV is more likely to develop serious infections, such as pneumonia, and other illnesses, including cancer. When this happens, they are said to have "advanced HIV infection" or AIDS (aquired immune deficiency syndrome).

How is HIV passed on?

HIV lives in body fluids such as semen, vaginal fluid and blood. There are two main ways in which it is passed from one person to another. One is when semen or vaginal fluid from an infected person enters another person's body during sexual activity. The other is when an infected person's blood gets into another person's body. For this reason, drug users who inject using shared equipment are at risk. Women with the virus can pass it on to their baby during pregnancy, at birth or in breast milk.

Medical research and HIV

Although there is no cure for HIV, a lot is known about it. Doctors can test a person's blood to see if it contains anti-HIV antibodies. If it does, the person is said to be "HIV positive".

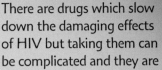
The HIV virus has spikes which allow it to grab onto and invade white blood cells.

There are drugs which slow down the damaging effects of HIV but taking them can be complicated and they are powerful, so often have side effects. Research is being done to try to produce more effective anti-HIV drugs and to develop a vaccine so that people could be immunized against it.

Preventing HIV

If a person's partner is infected with HIV, having vaginal or anal intercourse, or possibly oral sex (see the glossary) is risky. Using a condom helps to reduce the risk. Because of the risk of getting infected blood in the bloodstream, anything which punctures the skin is risky unless it has been sterilized. This includes all body-piercing equipment, as well as tattooing and acupuncture needles. Drug users should not share injecting equipment.

How HIV is not passed on

HIV only survives for a short time outside the body, so it is not passed on by ordinary everyday contact. You cannot get the virus by touching an infected person or objects used by them, such as towels or toilet seats. There is no known case of anyone getting the virus from saliva, for example by kissing or sharing crockery, or from tears or sweat, although these are all body fluids. It seems that, although the virus can live in these fluids, it cannot be passed on through them. Swimming pools are safe because the chemicals in the water kill the virus. In many countries, including Britain, needles and syringes used by medical staff are always either new or sterilized between patients, and all blood is tested for HIV before being given to anyone needing a transfusion.

Food

A healthy diet is important at any age but is especially necessary at puberty. The food you eat helps you to grow and gives you energy.

Different types of food do different jobs in your body so you need to eat a good balance of all the types. Water, too, is essential.

Protein

Over ten per cent of the human body is made of a substance called protein, and you need to eat protein to grow and for your body to repair itself. Protein is especially important at puberty, when you are growing and developing very fast. Good sources are lean meat, fish, cheese, eggs, milk, nuts and beans.

Fats

Fats give you some of your energy. There are two types: **saturated**, found in animal products such as meat, butter, cream and most margarines, and **unsaturated**, found in non-animal products such as liquid vegetable oils, certain margarines and spreads, and nuts. Too much saturated fat may contribute to heart disease.

Carbohydrates

Carbohydrates should provide most of your energy. There are two forms of carbohydrate: **starches** and **sugars**. It is better to eat starchy foods, such as bread, potatoes, rice and pasta, rather than sweet foods such as cakes, biscuits, chocolate and ice cream or sweetened drinks. Sugar is of no benefit to your body apart from giving you energy and it is bad for your teeth.

Fibre

Fibre is a type of carbohydrate that you can't digest but it is essential in your diet. It travels through your digestive tract in bulk, making the muscles of your intestines work efficiently, preventing constipation.

Fibre may also help prevent serious diseases of the intestines such as cancer. It is found in vegetables, fruit, wholemeal bread and pasta, wholegrain cereals, brown rice, lentils, beans and nuts.

Vitamins and minerals

You need small amounts of almost 40 different vitamins and minerals for essential chemical processes to take place in your body. Eat as wide a variety of healthy, fresh foods as you can to be sure of getting them all. People may sometimes benefit from taking a supplement too, as long as the dose is not too high.

Calcium is a mineral. It is found in foods such as milk and cheese and is important at puberty because it makes your bones and teeth strong.

Iron is a mineral which is essential for healthy blood. Women need more iron than men because they lose it when they have periods. It is found in foods such as meat, fish, eggs, some breakfast cereals and bread.

Salt is also an essential mineral, though people in developed countries usually eat much more of it than they need and this may play a part in heart disease.

A healthy balance

Dietitians divide food into five groups.

1. Bread, potatoes, cereals, rice and pasta (starchy carbohydrates) – eat lots of these.
2. Fruit and vegetables (fresh, frozen or canned) – eat five portions a day, more if you can. (Potatoes are not included in this group but beans and lentils are.)
3. Meat, fish, eggs, nuts, beans, lentils – eat in moderate amounts.
4. Milk, cheese, yogurt – eat in moderate amounts.
5. Foods containing fat and/or sugar – don't eat too many of these.

Vegetarian food

A vegetarian diet (one without meat or fish) has to be planned carefully to be healthy. Vegetarians must make sure they eat enough foods from group 3 above and need to know, for example, that iron from eggs and plant foods (instead of meat) needs vitamin C for their body to absorb it.

Processed food

Processed food is food that has been through an industrial process to alter it in some way. For example, it may have been heated, or chopped up and then re-formed into a whole. Most ready-made meals, for example, have been processed; so have bought burgers, pizzas, biscuits and cakes, and jars of sauce.

Processing can reduce the goodness in food. Also, the food often has substances added to it during the processing (see page 40).

Wholefoods such as wholegrain bread, pasta and rice go through less processing than white varieties.

Many dietitians think it best to eat food in the form as close to its natural, unprocessed state as possible. This includes "whole" foods.

It is also best to eat food as fresh as possible, because vitamins and minerals are lost, as food gets older.

Additives and pesticides

Organic food aims to be free from pesticides and additives but is expensive.

Many processed foods contain additives made from artificial substances. Some researchers think that certain artificial additives, for example some colourings and sweeteners, can cause ill health.

Pesticides are sprayed on crops to kill pests and many experts believe even small traces of these are harmful to humans too.

Junk food

Junk food is food with very little or no goodness in it. Usually it contains lots of sugar, fat, salt, or artificial additives such as colourings. It is often fattening too. Junk food includes sugary drinks, sweets, lollies, biscuits and salted snacks, including crisps.

To find out what is in your food, read the labels. Beware of foods with a lot of sugar, saturated fat or salt (sodium).

Rather than trying to avoid junk food altogether, you could try just eating it occasionally but have healthier snacks like fruit most of the time.

Is breakfast important?

Your body uses some energy even when you're asleep. In the morning, it needs food to kick-start it into action and to replace your energy store. People who eat breakfast have been shown to work more efficiently and with better concentration than those who don't.

Kilojoules

About 170 kJ   About 1000 kJ   About 4000 kJ

The amount of energy that can be produced from food is measured in kilojoules (kJ) or calories. Different foods have different numbers of kilojoules. How many kilojoules people need depends on how much energy they use up.

Male at puberty needs approximately 12,000 kJ a day.	Female at puberty needs approximately 9,000 kJ a day.

Going through puberty takes such a lot of energy that you need as many kilojoules then as a full-grown adult does. Males generally use more energy than females because they are bigger.

Weight

Your weight increases even more spectacularly than your height at puberty, as a result of your larger bones and internal organs, and increasing amounts of muscle and fat. The female sex hormones make females gain more fat than males. This is an energy store they can draw on during pregnancy. It isn't easy to suggest ideal weights, as people are different builds.

Age 10

46% of final weight   56% of final weight

Being overweight

Any kilojoules not used as energy are stored in your body as fat instead. On average, fat people die younger and suffer more from certain illnesses, including heart disease, than slimmer people. If you think you may be overweight, ask a doctor or dietitian. If you weigh over 13kg (29lb) more than the average weight of all your friends, you may be eating too many fattening foods.

The best way to lose weight is to cut down on fatty foods, especially fried foods such as chips, and sugary foods and drinks. Some foods, for example milk shakes, ice cream and biscuits, are mostly fat and sugar. Fibre will fill you up without making you fat. Don't go on an unusual or crash diet. These are unbalanced and you will probably put back the weight once you stop the diet.

Eating disorders

There are three main eating disorders: anorexia nervosa, bulimia nervosa and binge-eating disorder. They affect mainly girls but boys can suffer from them too.

Everyone overeats now and again but a sufferer from binge-eating disorder regularly eats unusually large amounts of food in a short time and feels that they can't stop themselves from doing it. Afterwards they feel ashamed of their overeating. Sufferers from this disorder can become very overweight.

Sufferers from anorexia become obsessed with losing weight, thinking they are fat when they are not. They eat so little that they become dangerously thin. Some sufferers may exercise obsessively.

Someone with bulimia is also very afraid of getting fat. Instead of not eating, they binge eat but then make themselves vomit or take laxatives so they don't put on weight. They may also starve themselves for a few days after bingeing.

Experts think that eating disorders are mainly psychological, but that they are also partly inherited. They may be triggered by stressful events in a person's life.

Sufferers generally have low self-esteem and use food as a way of trying to cope with painful situations and feelings, or to ease stress.

Many anorexics and bulimics say that, at first, rigidly controlling what they eat is a way of being in control of their lives, but that, in the end, it is the eating disorder which controls them.

Some people think that the fashion for thinness in Western society may contribute to the disorders; there are media images of thin celebrities all around and they are considered to have ideal bodies even when they are unhealthily thin.

Eating disorders are very serious, even life-threatening illnesses. Sufferers can experience a wide range of symptoms including stomach pains, spots, difficulty sleeping and irregular or no periods. They may become severely depressed, they may not grow and develop properly, important organs may be damaged, and some even die from malnutrition.

If you think you may have an eating disorder, it is vitally important to tell an adult you trust. If you think a friend of yours may have an eating disorder, try to tell them as gently as possible that you are worried about them and see if you can persuade them to tell an adult.

Most eating disorder sufferers respond well to treatment from a doctor or counsellor but the sooner they seek medical advice the easier it will be.

Exercise

Exercise is an essential part of good health. ẞy making sure you get plenty of exercise during puberty, you help your body to develop as fully as possible.

Exercise doesn't only make the muscles of your skeleton strong.

It also strengthens your heart, which is a muscle too, your lungs and your bones. The younger you are when you start getting fit, the easier it will be, and the more likely you are to avoid certain illnesses, especially heart disease, as you get older.

What can exercise do?

Exercise can have many benefits. Here are some of them.

1. Exercise makes you strong by increasing the size and strength of your muscles. Without it, muscles waste away.

2. It keeps your joints supple so they don't stiffen up and cause aches and pains.

3. It strengthens your heart so that it pumps blood more efficiently. This means it can do more work with less effort. Just running for a bus can strain an unfit person's heart.

4. It makes you breathe deeper and take in more oxygen. The food you eat must be combined with oxygen inside your body before it can give you energy.

5. It improves your circulation by making your blood vessels more elastic and opening up new channels. This means that food and oxygen, which are carried in your blood, get around your body more efficiently.

6. It improves your speed of reaction and coordination by making your brain and nervous system work more efficiently. It also helps you to move more gracefully.

7. It helps to keep you slim by using up kilojoules in your food.

8. It helps you relax and overcome stress. You feel generally healthier and happier.

What kind of exercise?

Almost any type of exercise is better than none at all, but for general health and fitness it is best to do a sport which has as many of the benefits shown above as possible. These include swimming, soccer, aerobics, energetic dancing, cycling and fast walking.

How much exercise?

Experts think you should exercise for at least half an hour every day. This sounds a lot but it can include walking, so long as you walk fast. At least twice a week, the exercise should be fairly strenuous. Exercising obsessively or when you are unwell can do more harm than good.

Rest

Rest can be physical relaxation such as sleep, or just a change of activity. After exercising hard, sitting and reading a book or watching television will rest your muscles and heart. After you have been studying hard, doing some kind of exercise will rest your brain.

Sleep

You will probably find you need quite a lot of sleep at puberty because you are growing fast and using up so much energy. Most 10-14 year-olds need about ten hours sleep a night and 14-18 year-olds about nine hours but it can vary. The best guide to how much sleep you need is the way you feel.

The reason for sleep is not really understood. During sleep, your muscles relax and your heart and breathing rates fall, so it may be a period of recovery and repair for the body. Dreaming may be a way of making sense of things that have happened to you, and part of learning.

Posture

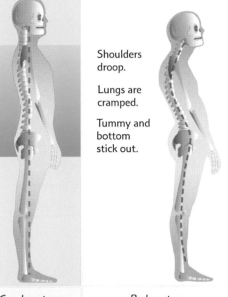

Shoulders droop.

Lungs are cramped.

Tummy and bottom stick out.

Good posture   Bad posture

Good posture is difficult to learn but once you know how to stand or sit properly, it is actually less tiring than slumping, as it places less strain on your body. Try to imagine a vertical line running through your pelvis from just behind your ear to just in front of your ankle, as shown in the diagram above left. The one above right shows the strain put on your body by standing badly.

Shoes

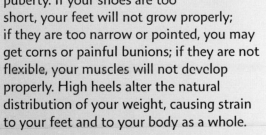

Your feet are not fully formed until you are about 20, so it is important to wear well-fitting shoes all the way through puberty. If your shoes are too short, your feet will not grow properly; if they are too narrow or pointed, you may get corns or painful bunions; if they are not flexible, your muscles will not develop properly. High heels alter the natural distribution of your weight, causing strain to your feet and to your body as a whole.

Drugs

Drugs are chemical substances which alter the way the body works. Some drugs are used to treat diseases; some are taken simply because they change the way people feel, think and behave. All drugs can be harmful, or deadly, if they are misused.

You are bound to be offered drugs at some time. The best way to avoid problems with them is simply not to take them.

Drugs and the law

There are lots of drugs that it is illegal to possess, sell or give to other people. The penalties for being caught with an illegal drug vary according to the drug and the country you are in. In Britain, for instance, the penalties range from having your name kept on police record for five years to going to prison for several years. Employers can check whether someone has a drugs' record and most will not give a job to anyone who does.

Legal drugs

Even pills, powders and other drugs which you can buy without a prescription, such as painkillers and cold remedies, can damage your health or even kill you, if you take too many, take them too often or mix them. They are all chemicals which are not natural to your body. If you have a headache, you could find that lying down and relaxing for a while might work just as well as a painkiller. You should never take any medicine which has been prescribed for someone else.

Types of drugs

Different drugs are taken in different ways: swallowed, sniffed, smoked or injected, and they have different effects.

Stimulants ("uppers") speed up people's bodies and make them feel energetic and excited. Examples of stimulants include cocaine, crack, ecstasy, poppers, speed and tobacco.

Depressants ("downers") slow people's bodies down and make them feel relaxed and drowsy. Alcohol, glues, gases, aerosols and heroin are examples of downers.

Hallucinogens or psychedelics send people on a "trip", distorting the way things normally appear. LSD and magic mushrooms are both hallucinogens.

Glue, gas and aerosols

Glue, gas and aerosols can all be misused.

Breathing in the chemicals in glue, lighter gas refills or aerosol sprays has a similar effect on the body to alcohol but is much more dangerous. There have been many cases of sudden death after sniffing, often because the heart is affected. Sniffing from a plastic bag can cause death by suffocation. Spraying the substances directly into the mouth can make the body produce fluid that floods the lungs and causes instant death. Some long-term sniffers suffer damage to their brain, liver or kidneys. It is especially dangerous to mix sniffing with drinking alcohol.

Cannabis

Cannabis is usually made into a joint or spliff with tobacco, so it looks a bit like a cigarette and is smoked.

It generally makes people feel relaxed, though it can make some people panicky or paranoid (imagining people are saying horrible things about them). Heavy users can become tired all the time and unable to concentrate, learn and work.

Cannabis is sold in two forms: resin (above and below) and leaf (right).

A spliff

Cannabis damages the lungs in a similar way to tobacco because it contains many of the same chemicals (see page 46). Other names for cannabis include dope, ganja, grass, hash, marijuana, pot, skunk and weed.

Health risks of drug-taking

There are many risks to taking drugs. No one can ever know for sure how a drug will affect them. The same drug can have a very different effect on different people, and even on the same person at different times. It is impossible to know how strong an illegal drug is or exactly what is in it, as the drug itself is often mixed with other substances. The large number of slang names for different drugs can be confusing and the names change often.

The bad effects of different drugs include feeling sick and dizzy, getting confused and so more accident-prone, feeling tired but unable to sleep, and feeling anxious, frightened or panicky. Some drugs, for example ecstasy, can kill even at the first dose and most drugs kill if someone takes too big a dose.

Mixing drugs is extremely dangerous and this includes mixing any other drug with alcohol.

Tolerance. If someone's body gets used to a drug (becomes tolerant to it), they start having to take larger and larger amounts of it to get the same effect. Taking larger amounts increases the risks involved.

Dependency. Many drugs can be habit-forming, so the person using them becomes dependent on them. The dependence, also known as addiction, may be psychological so that they feel they can't cope without the drug; or it may be physical, which means that their body gets used to having the drug and is disturbed without it. Either way, it can be very hard indeed to give drugs up. People trying to stop taking drugs can experience bad withdrawal symptoms such as shaking, anxiety, depression, panic attacks, insomnia and intense craving for the drug. It is impossible to know in advance who will and who won't become drug dependent.

Drug-taking can lead to all kinds of long-term problems - psychological as well as physical. Besides damaging people's health, it can ruin their relationships, affect their work and lead to them stealing to pay for their drugs.

Ecstasy tablets come in different sizes, shapes and colours (often white). Some have patterns on them.

Smoking and drinking

Both smoking and heavy drinking are bad for your health. They cause serious, even fatal illnesses. Nicotine (in tobacco) and alcohol are both addictive drugs. Nicotine is addictive even in small amounts.

Smoking

Smokers are less healthy than nonsmokers and most heavy smokers die of diseases caused by smoking. Nonsmokers are at risk just by being in a smoky atmosphere. It is always worth giving up smoking. Unless disease has already set in, the risks gradually decrease until, ten years after giving up, they almost disappear. Two of the most poisonous chemicals in tobacco are nicotine and tar.

Nicotine

Nicotine acts on the brain and nervous system and is what gives some smokers pleasure. It makes people unused to smoking feel faint and sick. Nicotine makes the heart beat faster and narrows the blood vessels, contributing to heart and circulatory disease.

Breathing in tar

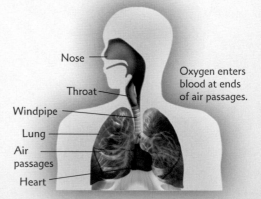

Nose
Throat
Windpipe
Lung
Air passages
Heart
Oxygen enters blood at ends of air passages.

The air you breathe has to be cleaned before it reaches the lowest part of your lungs. This is the purpose of the slippery liquid called mucus that you have in your nose and upper air passages. The mucus traps dirt and bacteria, while tiny hairs called cilia waft the mucus away from your lungs towards your nose and throat.

The tar in tobacco smoke irritates the air passages, making them narrower, increasing mucus production and making the cilia less efficient, so that the mucus, dirt and bacteria stay in the lungs. This causes "smoker's cough", which is really a symptom of bronchitis (inflammation of the air passages) and makes the lungs more prone to infection.

Smoking facts

- It is estimated that every cigarette shortens a smoker's life by 14 minutes.
- Half of all teenagers smoking today will die from diseases caused by tobacco if they continue to smoke. Half of these smokers will die early.
- One in every three cases of cancer is thought to be directly related to smoking.
- Nine out of ten cases of lung cancer occur in smokers.
- Most people who smoke wish they had never started.
- Smoking makes you smell.

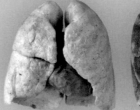
Healthy lung

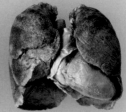
Smoker's lung blackened by tar

Alcohol

Alcohol is a depressant drug. Small doses can make people feel relaxed and confident. Larger doses slow their reactions and affect coordination and judgement. This makes them more likely to have an accident, and is why drinking and driving or riding a bike is dangerous. Alcohol also exaggerates emotions so people may do things they later regret, like getting into fights or having sex.

Someone who has drunk a lot may get sick and dizzy, or even fall unconscious, adding the danger of choking on vomit. Drinking a lot causes a hangover next day, which means a headache and feeling sick.

The effects of alcohol are increased if the drinker is not used to alcohol, if they have not eaten a meal recently, or if they drink fast. The person's size also counts: large people are usually more resistant to alcohol than small people.

Alcoholic content

The approximate amount of alcohol in different drinks

Spirits: 40%   Wine: 13%   Beer: 5%   Alcopops: 5%

The effects of drinking depend partly on how concentrated the alcohol is in the drink. In general, spirits, such as whisky or vodka, are the strongest, then wine, then beer and alcopops. The percentage of alcohol in a drink is given on its label.

Some governments advise a maximum number of alcoholic "units" that men and women can safely drink over the course of a week. It is easy to be confused by this, though, as the size of glasses varies.

Binge drinking

Binge drinking (drinking a large amount in one session, usually on purpose to get drunk) is especially dangerous for young people. It may damage your brain, which doesn't finish developing until your early 20s; it can affect learning and memory.

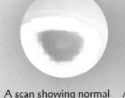

A scan showing normal brain activity

A scan showing reduced brain activity in an alcoholic

Long-term effects

The long-term effects of heavy drinking can include getting fat, as alcohol contains a lot of kilojoules; inflammation of the stomach; shrivelling and scarring of the liver (cirrhosis); some types of cancer; and damage to the brain, kidneys and muscles, including the heart. Heavy drinking also causes psychological and social problems, including damaging relationships and job prospects.

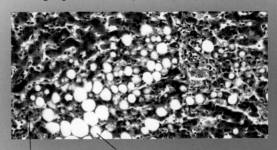

Normal liver cell   Liver cell damaged by alcohol

If someone regularly drinks heavily, their brain has to struggle against the depressant effect of the alcohol to keep them awake. If they then stop drinking, their brain continues compensating, which makes them excited, nervous, shaky and fidgety until they get another drink. This is an example of addiction.

Keeping clean

Keeping clean becomes more important at puberty than it was during childhood. Your skin starts producing more of the substances that can cause unpleasant smells or even bad health if you don't wash them off regularly.

Skin

The picture on the right shows a slice through your skin so you can see what it is like below the surface.

Surface skin: your surface skin is called the epidermis. Its top layer is dead and is constantly being worn away as you come into contact with things. It is replaced by skin from lower down in the epidermis.

Sebaceous glands: these produce an oily substance called sebum, which coats your hair and skin, helping to keep them waterproof and supple. At puberty, the sebaceous glands start producing more sebum and this can sometimes cause greasy hair and spots.

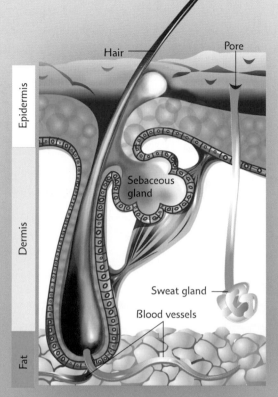

Hair · Pore · Epidermis · Sebaceous gland · Dermis · Sweat gland · Blood vessels · Fat

Sweat glands: even when you aren't hot, sweat is constantly coming up to the surface of your skin from your sweat glands and coming out through your pores. The sweat helps to rid your body of waste and keep your temperature stable. At puberty, you start to sweat more.

Washing

You need to wash every day to get rid of dirt, dead skin, sebum and sweat. Your sweat glands are most numerous under your arms and around your genitals, so it is important to wash these parts of your body every day, even if you don't have an all-over shower.

Armpits

All the sweat glands under your arms can make you sweat a lot, especially if you are excited or nervous. Using a deodorant or antiperspirant helps to stop smells developing before you have a chance to wash. Deodorants work by slowing down the growth of bacteria on the sweat and antiperspirants make you sweat less by closing some of your pores.

48

Teeth

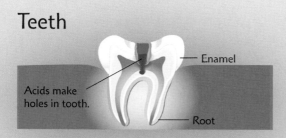

Enamel

Acids make holes in tooth.

Root

Most people have all their adult teeth by about age 13, except for the four wisdom teeth, which come through later. To prevent tooth and gum disease, you need to brush your teeth at least twice a day.

Tooth decay is caused by bacteria which feed on sugar in your mouth. They multiply and form a substance called plaque. This contains acids, which eat holes into the tooth. If these aren't filled, the tooth starts to ache, and an infection or abscess may develop. The tooth may work loose if the gum is damaged.

It is important to go to the dentist regularly. You can help by eating and drinking less sugar and by using fluoride toothpaste, which strengthens your teeth.

How to clean your teeth

Brush up and down, not from side to side.

It is important to clean your teeth thoroughly rather than vigorously. Brush up and down, not across, with small strokes, so that the bristles get between your teeth. Work your way right around your mouth and brush the backs of your teeth as well as the fronts. For this, it is easiest to hold the brush vertically. Don't rush. It is unhygienic to use anyone else's toothbrush (see also page 36).

Genitals

Urine, vaginal fluids, period blood, semen and smegma are all clean, though once they leave your body, bacteria can breed on them, as well as on the sweat produced in the area. Bacteria can get into your body through the vagina, urethral opening or penis, so you need to wash your genital area every day. The rectum contains many bacteria, so it is important, especially for females, to wash and dry from front to back, to avoid spreading them to the nearby vagina or urethra. Males need to roll back their foreskin and wash gently underneath. Wash with mild soap and warm water, but don't use deodorants or perfumes: they can cause irritation. After washing, put on clean underwear.

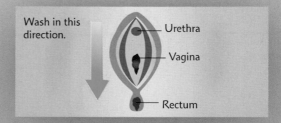

Wash in this direction.

Urethra

Vagina

Rectum

Discharges

A certain amount of vaginal discharge is normal. It is just the cleansing and lubricating fluids from the cervix and vagina leaking out. The fluids vary from clear to milky and have almost no smell. Some girls have a heavier discharge for a few months before their periods start.

If your normal discharge becomes a lot heavier or thicker, changes colour, or starts to smell, itch or burn, it probably means that normally harmless bacteria in the vagina have got out of hand and you have an infection. The doctor will be able to treat it with pessaries or tablets. Males should go to the doctor if they have any discharge at all from their penis.

Face

Many experts say that soap is bad for your face because it is a detergent and can dry up sebum too much. On the other hand, people at puberty tend to have too much sebum anyway and you may find that the cleansing creams and lotions you can buy give you spots. The best thing to do is work out what suits your particular skin. If your spots are very bad, it is worth going to the doctor's.

Spots

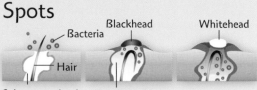

Bacteria · Blackhead · Whitehead · Hair · Sebaceous gland · Trapped sebum

It is changes in hormone levels during puberty that can make your sebaceous glands produce too much sebum. The glands are most numerous on your face and back. Testosterone is probably the hormone most involved, so spots, or acne, are more common in males than females.

If the sebum accumulates at the opening of a sebaceous gland, you get a blackhead.

If the sebum builds up below the surface of the skin, you get a whitehead or a reddish lump. The spot may be infected by bacteria.

If you are prone to spots, try washing your face often using mild, unperfumed or antiseptic soap and warm water. Males can try wiping their razor with liquid antiseptic after shaving. Some people try to camouflage spots with make-up, but this usually only makes them worse.

You shouldn't really squeeze spots, because of the risk of damaging your skin and spreading any infection. If you do squeeze, make sure your hands are very clean and try only to squeeze blackheads.

Hair

Your hair needs to be washed to clear it of dirt, dead cells, sebum and sweat. The amount of sebum you produce determines whether you have dry or greasy hair. Greasy hair may need to be washed every day, dry hair much less often. Dandruff consists of dead cells from the head. It is more likely to affect people with dry hair. Alternating the makes of shampoo that you use can be the best remedy. If the dandruff gets very bad, go to the doctor.

Nails

Right way to cut your big toenail.　　Wrong way to cut your big toenail.

Keep your nails clean by scrubbing underneath with a nail brush. You can cut your finger nails with scissors or nail clippers, or file them with an emery board. Metal files tend to split the nails. If your nails break easily, keep them short.

For your toenails, you need very sharp scissors. Cut the nails straight across. Shaping them can make the edges grow into the flesh and, if they break the skin, cause infection. This is an ingrown toenail.

Your feelings

As you mature physically and emotionally, you become more independent and your relationships with the people around you alter. Some people find these changes stressful at times. It may help to remember that other people are experiencing the same thing, and that older people once went through similar experiences. The way you feel may be affected by physical changes in your body, over which you have no control.

Independence

As you grow up, you will probably want to take more responsibility for your own life and actions. This can cause conflict with your parents, who have to adjust to the idea of you becoming more independent.

Identity

Thinking about what kind of person you are and what you want to do and be in the future is an important part of growing up. It can feel confusing sometimes, coming to terms with your adult personality.

Friends

Most teenagers make close friends and some even fall in love. You may have a group of friends, but beware of feeling you must always do what the others do, especially if you feel uncomfortable about it.

Moods

At times, you may feel moody and irritable without really knowing why. Changes in your hormone levels can be partly to blame. Things usually improve as you get used to your adult body and feelings.

Shyness

Many adolescents suffer from shyness, lacking confidence in their personality and looks. How you cope depends on your individual character. Remember that others often feel shy even if they don't look it.

Glossary

Here are some words you may hear whose meanings you don't know. If the word you want is not listed below, try looking in the index at the back of this book, as it may be explained elsewhere.

Acne. The condition of having lots of spots, usually on the face, chest, back or shoulders. It is a combination of inflamed and pus-containing spots and blackheads, probably caused by hormone activity.

Adultery. Sexual intercourse between a person who is married and someone who is not their husband or wife.

Amenorrhoea. Absence of periods.

Anal intercourse. Intercourse in which the penis enters the rectum (back passage).

Androgynous. Looking partly male and partly female in appearance.

Aphrodisiac. A substance which increases sexual desire.

Birth control. Contraception.

BO. Body odour, caused by not washing often enough, or not using deodorant.

Brothel. House where prostitutes have sex with their clients.

Calendar method. Unreliable method of contraception which involves predicting a "safe period" for intercourse from the dates of the woman's periods.

Castration. Removal of a male's testicles.

Celibacy. Not having sexual intercourse for a longish period of time.

Chastity. Virginity (see page 54) or celibacy.

Child abuse. Mistreating a child, that is anyone under 16, including forcing or persuading her/him into sexual activity. In many countries, including Britain, this is illegal and there are organizations which help children who are being mistreated, or who have been mistreated in the past (see the end of the book).

Clap. Slang word for gonorrhoea (see below).

Coitus. Sexual intercourse.

Copulation. Sexual intercourse.

Crabs. Pubic lice (see page 54).

Cystitis. Inflammation of the bladder, which causes pain when going to the toilet. Cystitis is usually caused by bacterial infection and is more common in females than males.

Erotic. To do with sexual love; producing sexual desire.

Family planning. Contraception; birth control.

Feminist. Someone who wants to improve the rights and lives of women.

Flasher. Someone who displays their genitals in public.

Gonorrhoea. One of the most common sexually transmitted diseases. It can usually be cured by antibiotics but there may be no symptoms in women and they may become infertile (see page 53).

Grooming. Gaining the trust of a child, often on the Internet, with the aim of sexually abusing them.

Gynaecologist. Doctor who specializes in diseases of the female reproductive system.

Herpes (genital). Also called herpes type 2. A sexually transmitted infection for which no cure is yet known. There is no connection between genital herpes and herpes simplex (herpes type 1), which is a cold sore.

Homophobia. Hatred or fear of homosexuals.

Hysterectomy. Operation to remove a woman's uterus.

Impotence. Inability of a male to get an erection or have an orgasm.

Incest. Sexual intercourse between two people who are too closely related to be allowed to be legally married, e.g. father/daughter, uncle/niece, brother/sister. In many countries, including ßritain, incest is illegal and the law also applies to step relations and foster carers.

Infertility. Inability to have children.

Libido. Sex drive.

Masochist. Someone who gets pleasure from having pain inflicted on them.

Menstruate. To have periods, or a period.

Missionary position. A position for sexual intercourse with the couple lying facing each other, the man on top.

Molest. To make unwanted sexual advances to someone.

Monogamy. Having a sexual relationship with only one person over a period of time.

NSU (Non-specific urethritis). Inflammation of the urethra - the tube leading from the bladder to the outside of the body. This is a sexually transmitted infection which affects males only.

Nymphomaniac. Woman who has a compulsion to have sex with as many men as possible but without having lasting relationships with them.

Oral sex. Stimulation of the genitals by mouth.

Paedophile. Adult who is sexually attracted to children.

Penetrative sex. Vaginal or anal intercourse.

Perversion. Abnormal sexual activity.

Phallus. Image of an erect penis. If something is described as phallic, it resembles an erect penis.

Platonic (friendship). Nonsexual.

Pornography. Pictures or writing aimed at producing sexual arousal.

Pox. Slang word for syphilis (see page 54).

Premature ejaculation. Male orgasm reached too quickly.

Promiscuity. Sexual intercourse with several different casual acquaintances over a short period of time.

Prostitute. Person who has sex with someone in return for payment.

Pubic lice. A sexually transmitted disease caused by a blood-sucker called the crab louse which lives in pubic hair.

Rape. Forcing someone to have sexual intercourse, vaginal or anal, against their will.

Reproduction. Production of offspring.

Sadist. Someone who gets pleasure from inflicting pain.

Safe sex. Protecting yourself and your partner against sexually transmitted infections and pregnancy, for example by using condoms.

Sexist. Someone who thinks people should behave in a certain way because of their gender (which sex they are).

Sexual harassment. Making of unwanted sexual advances to someone; molesting.

Sixty-nine. Simultaneous oral stimulation of the genitals, so-called because of the position of the couple's bodies. (Also referred to in French as soixante-neuf.)

Snogging. Sexual contact which involves kissing and touching the partner's body but does not include intercourse.

Sodomy. Anal intercourse.

Solicit. To approach people in public places offering sex in return for payment.

Sterilization. A surgical operation to make someone permanently incapable of having children. Generally, people are only sterilized if they already have children and are certain they don't want any more. Male sterilization is easier to do than female.

Syphilis. A very serious sexually transmitted disease which can be cured by antibiotics.

Temperature method. Unreliable method of contraception which involves predicting a "safe period" for intercourse from changes in the woman's temperature during her period cycle.

Testes. Testicles.

Thrush (candidiasis). A common sexually transmitted disease which can develop without sexual contact. It is caused by a yeast fungus. Symptoms occur mainly in women and include increased vaginal discharge, itching, or pain when going to the toilet. Treatment is with anti-fungal pessaries or pills, and sometimes cream for the male partner.

Transsexual. Someone who wants to change sex or who has had a sex change operation.

Transvestite. Someone who wears clothes of the opposite sex; a cross-dresser.

Vasectomy. Male sterilization.

Virgin. Someone who has never had sexual intercourse.

Voyeur. Someone who gets sexual pleasure from secretly watching other people's sexual activities or from secretly watching people undressing; a peeping tom.

Whore. Prostitute.

Withdrawal method. A completely unreliable method of contraception in which the man withdraws his penis from the vagina before he ejaculates.

Index

Acknowledgements

Managing designer: Mary Cartwright. Cover design: Nancy Leschnikoff.
Photographic manipulation: Emma Julings and Nancy Leschnikoff.

Photo credits

The publishers are grateful to the following for permission to reproduce material:
Cover © Royalty-free/CORBIS; **page 5 (bottom right)** © Innerspace Imaging/Science Photo Library; **page 11 (top right)** © Michael W. Davidson/Science Photo Library, (bottom right) © Susumu Nishinaga/Science Photo Library; **page 15 (bottom left)** © Science Photo Library; **page 21 (top right)** © Professor P. M. Motta, G. Macchiarelli, S. A. Nottola/Science Photo Library; **page 25 (bottom right)** © Alfred Pasieka/Science Photo Library; **page 36** © D. Phillips/Science Photo Library; **page 45 (top right)** © Alex Tossi/Alamy, (bottom right) © Martin Norris/Alamy; **page 46 (bottom, both lungs)** © Institut für Plastination Heidelberg, Germany (www.bodyworlds.com); **page 47 (top right)** © Leonard Lessin, Peter Arnold Inc./Science Photo Library, **(bottom right)** © Astrid and Hanns-Frieder Michler/Science Photo Library.

Every effort has been made to trace and acknowledge ownership of copyright. If any rights have been omitted, the publishers offer to rectify this in any subsequent editions following notification.